Sports Fun!

Skiing

by Kieran Downs

BLASTOFF! Beginners

BELLWETHER MEDIA
MINNEAPOLIS, MN

Blastoff! Beginners are developed by literacy experts and educators to meet the needs of early readers. These engaging informational texts support young children as they begin reading about their world. Through simple language and high frequency words paired with crisp, colorful photos, Blastoff! Beginners launch young readers into the universe of independent reading.

Sight Words in This Book

a	he	other	this
and	in	people	time
do	is	some	to
down	it	the	use
go	jump	their	we
got	on	they	will

This edition first published in 2024 by Bellwether Media, Inc.

Library of Congress Cataloging-in-Publication Data

Names: Downs, Kieran, author.
Title: Skiing / by Kieran Downs.
Description: Minneapolis, MN : Bellwether Media, 2024. | Series: Blastoff! beginners. Sports fun! | Includes bibliographical references and index. | Audience: Ages 4-7 | Audience: Grades K-1
Identifiers: LCCN 2023035138 (print) | LCCN 2023035139 (ebook) | ISBN 9798886877687 (library binding) | ISBN 9798886878622 (ebook)
Subjects: LCSH: Skis and skiing--Juvenile literature.
Classification: LCC GV854.315 .D68 2024 (print) | LCC GV854.315 (ebook) | DDC 796.93--dc23/eng/20230807
LC record available at https://lccn.loc.gov/2023035138
LC ebook record available at https://lccn.loc.gov/2023035139

Editor: Christina Leaf Designer: Gabriel Hilger

Printed in the United States of America, North Mankato, MN.

Table of Contents

Let's Ski!

It snowed.
We will go ski!

What Is Skiing?

Skiing is
a winter sport.
People move
on skis.

Some people
ski on teams.
Others ski alone.

Some people **cross-country** ski. They ski across land.

cross-country skiing

Some people ski down hills.

downhill skiing

On Skis

Skiers use
skis and poles.
Boots keep skis
on their feet.

pole

Some skiers race.
They ski fast
to the finish.

50 km
marathon
RYBINSK
1926
30 km
Demino
marathon
RYBINSK
1935

This skier is in a **course**. He got a fast time!

course

Freestyle skiers do jumps. They do tricks! Wow!

Skiing Facts

Skiing

Kinds of Skiing

cross-country skiing

downhill skiing

freestyle skiing

Glossary

course

an area that skiers race in

cross-country

a kind of skiing in which skiers go across land

freestyle

a kind of skiing in which skiers do tricks

To Learn More

ON THE WEB

FACTSURFER

Factsurfer.com gives you a safe, fun way to find more information.

1. Go to www.factsurfer.com.
2. Enter "skiing" into the search box and click 🔍.
3. Select your book cover to see a list of related content.

Index

The images in this book are reproduced through the courtesy of: Nuclear-lily, front cover, p. 1; BigTunaOnline, p. 3; MaszaS, p. 4; Ski_Baby, pp. 4-5; Billion Photos, p. 6; manonallard, pp. 6-7; ronniechua, pp. 8-9; Hero Images, p. 10; OldStory, pp. 10-11; Microgen, p. 12; Design Pics Inc/ Alamy, pp. 12-13; Hintau Aliaksei, p. 14; gorillaimages, pp. 14-15; Evegeny Biyatov/ AP Images, pp. 16-17; ultramarinfoto, pp. 18-19; Rades, pp. 20-21; FamVeld, p. 22 (skiing, downhill skiing); Levranii, p. 22 (cross-country skiing); tatyana_tomsickova, p. 22 (freestyle skiing); Ruslan Kudrin, p. 23 (course); Old Story, p. 23 (cross-country); JulPo, p. 23 (freestyle).